The Hilari Grandparent Handbook

Steve Lewis

About the Author:
Steve Lewis is a retired software engineer and lighthouse keeper who moved to the peaceful beaches of Gabriola Island, British Columbia. He has been a Foster Parent for special needs children for many years and has run a dog rescue with his wife Susan, rehoming dogs from Cuba, California and Mexico. Steve, a prolific book author and publisher, has embraced a vigorous second act and is currently living in a wonderful coastal home.

ABOUT
STEVE LEWIS

Adventure and Wanderlust: Steve loves spending time with his granddaughter Dayva and setting out on fascinating domestic and international travels with his cherished wife Susan. Their adventures on the road serve as an inspiration for his writing and give each piece of literature a unique flair.

Steve Lewis's books offer a wide selection to fit every interest, whether you're looking for a colorful escape, a tool for orderly living, a culinary adventure, or a shared family experience. Enter his world, where retirement serves as a blank canvas for ingenuity, discovery, and limitless opportunities. Go through Steve's books on Amazon to start the adventure.

Being a grandparent is like being a kid again, but with better snacks and fewer curfews. In these pages, we'll guide you through the laughter-filled journey of grandparenthood, offering tips, tricks, and a hefty dose of humor to make this chapter of your life one for the record books.

Remember, you've earned your stripes as a grandparent, so let's embrace the chaos and celebrate the joys together!

The Hilarious
Grandparent Handbook

Steve Lewis

Introduction:

Welcome to "The Hilarious Grandparent Handbook!"

Being a grandparent is like being a kid again, but with better snacks and fewer curfews. In these pages, we'll guide you through the laughter-filled journey of grandparenthood, offering tips, tricks, and a hefty dose of humor to make this chapter of your life one for the record books.

Remember, you've earned your stripes as a grandparent, so let's embrace the chaos and celebrate the joys together!

The Hilarious Grandparent Handbook

Chapter 1: The Grandparent Glossary

Before we dive headfirst into the world of grandparenting, let's start with some essential vocabulary.

Learn how to decipher grandkid lingo, from "Yeet" to "FOMO," so you're not left scratching your head during your next family gathering.

We'll also discuss the mysterious language of "parent-speak" – those cryptic phrases that indicate when it's time to back off and when it's time to lend a hand.

The Hilarious Grandparent Handbook

The Hilarious Grandparent Handbook Glossary

Yeet-a-saurus: A grandparent who tries to stay updated with the latest trends and slang but often gets it hilariously wrong.

FOMO (Fear of Missing Out): The nagging feeling that you're missing out on precious grandkid moments when you're not around.

Parent-speak: The mysterious language used by parents to communicate, often filled with coded phrases like, "We'll see," "Because I said so," and "Maybe later." Embarro-saurus: A grandparent who excels at embarrassing their grandkids with their antics and stories.

Giggly Goulash: A specialty dish cooked by a grandparent that is both delicious and laughter-inducing.
Groovy Grilled Cheese: A grandparent's twist on the classic grilled cheese sandwich, packed with extra love and a dash of unexpected ingredients.

Crafty Connoisseur: A grandparent who's an expert at crafting chaos during creative activities with their grandkids. Fleece Fortress: A blanket fort constructed by a grandparent, providing a cozy hideaway for imaginative playtime.

The Hilarious Grandparent Handbook

Grand-wear: The stylish yet sometimes eccentric clothing choices of a grandparent, often including Hawaiian shirts and quirky hats.

Storytelling Sage: A grandparent with a gift for spinning imaginative and humorous bedtime stories for their grandkids.

Adventure Artist: A grandparent who excels at planning and participating in memorable, laugh-inducing adventures with their grandkids.

Dance Diva: A grandparent who loves to break out their best dance moves and challenge their grandkids to a dance-off.

Sanity Saver: A clever trick or piece of advice that helps a grandparent keep their wits about them when the grandkids are running wild.

Legacy of Laughter: The goal of every grandparent to leave behind a treasure trove of love, wisdom, and, of course, laughter for their grandkids.

Grandparent Time Capsule: A special collection of mementos, stories, and keepsakes created by a grandparent to be passed down through generations.

The Hilarious Grandparent Handbook

Coolest Grandparent Competition: The informal contest among grandparents to maintain their title as the hippest and most fun grandparent in the family.

Hawaiian Shirt Parade: An event where all the grandkids and grandparents wear their most colorful and outlandish Hawaiian shirts, causing hilarity and chaos.

Naptime Ninja: A grandparent who excels at getting their grandkids to take naps, often through humor and creative bedtime routines.

Wisecrack Whisperer: A grandparent with a talent for delivering puns, dad jokes, and one-liners that leave the grandkids in stitches.

"Back in My Day" Chronicle: The stories and anecdotes told by a grandparent to illustrate how life was different when they were kids, often involving tales of walking uphill both ways to school.

Remember, being a grandparent is all about fun, love, and creating memories. Use this glossary to navigate the hilarious world of grandparenthood and keep those grandkid giggles coming!

The Hilarious Grandparent Handbook

Chapter 2: The Art of Embarrassing Your Grandkids

Grandparents have a sacred duty to embarrass their grandchildren, and we'll show you how to do it with style.

Discover the fine line between hilarious and cringe-worthy antics.

From dancing in public to sharing embarrassing stories from your past, you'll be a pro at making your grandkids roll their eyes and laugh uncontrollably.

The Hilarious Grandparent Handbook

The Art of Embarrassing Your Grandkids

Silly Stories: Create imaginative and silly stories together. You can take turns adding ridiculous elements or characters to the story to make them laugh.

Dad Jokes: Share some classic "dad jokes" or puns. Kids often enjoy groaning at these corny jokes, and it can be a fun bonding experience.

Funny Faces: Make funny faces or use props like fake mustaches, oversized glasses, or clown noses to create laughter and capture silly photos.

Dance Off: Have a dance-off where you show off your "unique" dance moves. Encourage your grandkids to join in, and enjoy the laughter together.

Play Dress-Up: Put on costumes and dress up as different characters or even each other. This can lead to lots of laughter and imaginative play.

Create "Grandma/Grandpa's Club": Invent a special club or secret handshake that only you and your grandkids can be part of. Share "club" activities and inside jokes.

The Hilarious Grandparent Handbook

Tongue Twisters: Challenge each other with tongue twisters or create your own. It can be a fun and entertaining way to improve language skills and share a laugh.

Exaggerated Storytelling: Tell exaggerated and humorous versions of family stories or
adventures, turning everyday events into epic tales.

Puppet Show: Use puppets or dolls to put on a funny puppet show or skit.
Kids love watching puppets come to life and tell amusing
stories.

Funny Food Creations: Get creative in the kitchen by making funny, whimsical food
creations together.
Try making smiley face pancakes or playful sandwiches.
Remember that the key is to have fun together and create
positive memories.

Always be attuned to your grandkids' reactions and make
sure they're comfortable with the level of humor and playfulness you're engaging in. If they ever express discomfort, it's important to respect their feelings and adjust your approach accordingly.

The goal is to build a strong and loving relationship filled
with laughter and joy.

The Hilarious Grandparent Handbook

Chapter 3: Grandparent's Gourmet:

Cooking for the Grandkids Cooking for your grandkids can be a delightful adventure, whether it's whipping up gourmet dishes or perfecting the art of mac 'n' cheese.

We'll provide easy and humorous recipes for grandparent- approved treats, like "Grandma's Giggly Goulash" and "Grandpa's Groovy Grilled Cheese."

The Hilarious Grandparent Handbook

Silly Face Pancakes: Make regular pancakes and let the grandkids use ingredients like chocolate chips, berries, and whipped cream to create funny faces on their pancakes. You can call them "Pancake Picasso" or "Emoji Pancakes."

Spaghetti Monsters: Cook spaghetti and let the grandkids add meatballs for eyes
and olives for mouths. These spaghetti monsters are deliciously spooky.

Ants on a Log: Spread peanut butter or cream cheese on celery sticks and
top them with raisins. Tell your grandkids they're eating

"logs with ants." It's a healthy and amusing snack.
Wacky Mini Pizzas:
Provide small pizza crusts and an assortment of toppings
like gummy worms, marshmallows, and gummy bears. Let
the grandkids create their crazy mini pizzas.

Pretzel Rod Fishing:
Dip pretzel rods into melted chocolate and let the grandkids add gummy fish as if they're fishing. A fun, edible
fishing expedition!

Fruit Kabob Swords:
Thread chunks of colorful fruits (pineapple, strawberries,
melon) onto wooden skewers. Call them "fruit kabob swords" and let the grandkids duel with their fruity weapons.

The Hilarious Grandparent Handbook

Funny Face Sandwiches: Create sandwiches with funny faces using ingredients like cheese slices for eyes, carrot sticks for a nose, and red bell pepper strips for a smile.

Ladybug Grapes: Make ladybug snacks by halving grapes, using cream cheese
as the "glue" to stick them together, and adding blueberry
spots for ladybug markings.

"Octo-dogs": Cut hot dogs into long, thin strips, leaving one end uncut.
When you boil or cook them, the strips will curl, resembling octopus legs.

Banana Ghosts: Peel bananas, dip them in white chocolate, and add chocolate chip eyes. These spooky banana ghosts are a fun twist on a classic treat.

Dinosaur Eggs": Make deviled eggs but call them "dinosaur eggs." Add a drop of green food coloring to the filling to make them look prehistoric.

Popcorn Surprise: Sneak some small candies or mini marshmallows into a bowl of popcorn and watch your grandkids' surprise when they find the hidden treasures.

The Hilarious Grandparent Handbook

Chapter 4: Crafting Chaos:

Creative Activities for Grandparents Craft time is a must for any grandparent handbook.

We'll guide you through simple, fun projects to keep your grandkids entertained and make cherished memories.

From finger painting to building a blanket fort, you'll be the Picasso of playtime in no time.

The Hilarious Grandparent Handbook

Sock Puppets: Create funny sock puppets by decorating old socks with googly eyes, buttons, and felt to make characters with quirky personalities.

Paper Plate Masks: Use paper plates, paint, markers, and other craft supplies to make hilarious masks that you can wear and have a mini masquerade party.

Funny Face Plant Pots: Paint clay pots with silly faces, and then plant small flowers or succulents in them to give them quirky hairdos.

Toilet Paper Roll Characters: Turn empty toilet paper rolls into funny characters by adding googly eyes, paper cutouts, and colorful paint.

Pasta Art: Create art using various pasta shapes, glue, and paint. Make pasta animals, cars, or any other fun design.
Junk Robot Sculptures: Collect old bits of broken toys, buttons, and other odds and ends to create whimsical and goofy robot sculptures.

Beaded Jewelry: Make funny and unique jewelry using colorful beads, strings, and charms. Create silly necklaces, bracelets, and earrings.

Handprint Animals: Trace your hands on paper, cut them out, and then turn them into hilarious animals by adding features like googly eyes and funny mouths.

The Hilarious Grandparent Handbook

Pine Cone Critters: Gather pine cones and decorate them with tiny hats, wiggly eyes, and pipe cleaner arms to make adorable critters.

Crazy Hat Day: Host a "Crazy Hat Day" where you and your grandkids decorate ordinary hats with feathers, stickers, glitter, and more for a fun and wacky headwear competition.

Recycled Robot Sculptures: Use old cardboard boxes, bottles, and other recyclable materials to create comical robots with moving parts.

Thumbprint Art: Make thumbprint animals, aliens, or characters with colorful ink or paint, turning each fingerprint into a funny, unique creation.

Funny T-shirt Designs: Create custom T-shirts with fabric markers and paints, designing humorous slogans or drawings.

Duct Tape Creations: Craft wallets, bags, or other items out of colorful duct tape, adding a fun twist to practical accessories.

Funny Family Portraits: Draw caricatures or exaggerated portraits of each family member, turning them into humorous keepsakes.

Mosaic Masterpieces: Craft quirky mosaic art using small, colorful tiles or broken pieces of old dishes.

The Hilarious Grandparent Handbook

Fruit and Vegetable Stamps: Cut fruits and veggies into funny shapes and use them as stamps to create unique prints and artwork.

Paper Bag Puppets: Decorate paper bags with markers, buttons, and fabric scraps to make entertaining puppets for impromptu shows.

Crazy Hair Day: Experiment with colorful hair chalk, temporary hair dye, or even wigs for a wacky "Crazy Hair Day" together.

Funny Fortune Tellers: Create funny fortune tellers (also known as cootie catchers) filled with silly predictions and challenges for each other.

These craft activities provide opportunities for laughter, creativity, and bonding between grandparents and their grandchildren. Have fun getting crafty and making lasting memories!

The Hilarious Grandparent Handbook

Chapter 5: Grandparent Fashion:

Rocking the Granny & Gramps Style Who says you can't be stylish and a grandparent at the same time?

We'll explore the world of grandparent fashion, from Hawaiian shirts to eccentric hats.

You'll be turning heads (and possibly raising eyebrows) at the next family gathering.

The Hilarious Grandparent Handbook

Velcro sneakers with socks: Grandparents often opt for the convenience of Velcro sneakers, and they pair them with knee-high socks for added comfort and support.

Fanny packs: Fanny packs have made a comeback, but grandparents have been rocking these practical waist pouches for years. They're perfect for carrying essentials like tissues and hard candies.

Hawaiian shirts: Bright and colorful Hawaiian shirts are a grandparent staple, and they're often worn for every occasion, from family gatherings to casual outings.

Cardigans and sweater vests: Grandparents love their cozy knitwear, and they're not afraid to layer a cardigan over a sweater vest for extra warmth. High-waisted pants:

Grandparents often prefer high- waisted pants for both comfort and style. These pants provide ample room for movement and are often paired with tucked-in shirts.

Oversized sunglasses: Grandparents love their oversized sunglasses, which not only protect their eyes but also add a touch of glamour to their look.

Bucket hats: The iconic bucket hat is a go-to accessory for many grandparents, providing sun protection and style in one.

The Hilarious Grandparent Handbook

Patterned scrunchies and hair accessories: Grandmothers often sport colorful and patterned scrunchies and hairpins to keep their hair in check.

Patterned muumuus and housedresses: For ultimate comfort and ease of movement, grandmothers opt for patterned muumuus and housedresses that are both stylish and practical.

Crocheted vests and shawls: Many grandparents are skilled at crocheting and often showcase their handiwork by wearing crocheted vests and shawls.
Bolo ties: Grandfathers, in particular, may be seen wearing bolo ties, often adorned with unique and ornate designs.

Large, round eyeglasses: Oversized, round eyeglasses are a classic choice for grandparents, adding a touch of vintage charm to their look.

Patterned compression stockings: For both fashion and health, patterned compression stockings are a common choice for grandparent fashion.

The Hilarious Grandparent Handbook

Sensible sun hats: Grandparents know the importance of sun protection, so they often don wide-brimmed, practical sun hats for outdoor activities.

Suspenders: Grandfathers often opt for suspenders, which not only keep their pants in place but also add a touch of old-school charm to their outfits.

Remember, fashion is subjective, and what might seem funny to some can be a source of comfort and style for others.

These fashion choices are a testament to the individuality and personality of our beloved grandparents.

The Hilarious Grandparent Handbook

Chapter 6: Storytime Shenanigans

Grandparents have a knack for telling the best bedtime stories, and we've got a guide to help you craft epic tales.

Learn how to incorporate grandparent wisdom and a dash of absurdity into your narratives.

We'll also provide a list of classic children's books to read aloud with a humorous twist.

The Hilarious Grandparent Handbook

Bedtime Rap: Tell the story in a rhythmic, rhyming style, like a rap song. Use a silly beat and get the kids to nod their heads to the story.

Bedtime Puppet Show: Use hand puppets or stuffed animals to act out the story. Give the characters funny voices and personalities.

Bedtime News Broadcast: Present the story as if it's breaking news, complete with an anchor's voice and humorous commentary on the events of the story.

 Bedtime Mystery: Make the story a detective mystery where the kids have to solve a hilarious and nonsensical case.

Bedtime "Choose Your Adventure": Let the kids make choices at different points in the story, leading to unexpected and funny outcomes.

Bedtime Bedtime: Start the story with "Once upon a bedtime," and turn common bedtime routines into a comical adventure.

Bedtime Stand-Up Comedy: Tell the story in the style of a stand-up comedian, incorporating jokes and one-liners throughout.

Bedtime Superhero: Turn the kids into superheroes in the story, complete with funny superpowers and hilarious villains.

The Hilarious Grandparent Handbook

Bedtime Fairy Tale Remix: Take a classic fairy tale and give it a modern and funny twist. For example, "The Three Little Pigs and the Big Bad Wolf's Failed Construction Business."

Bedtime Space Adventure: Set the story in outer space with funny aliens, spaceships, and intergalactic mishaps.

Bedtime Cooking Show: Present the story as if you're cooking up a delicious bedtime tale, complete with humorous ingredients and cooking instructions.

Bedtime Animal Tale: Tell the story from the perspective of a funny animal character, with their quirky take on human activities.

Bedtime Time-Travel Adventure: Send the kids on a wacky time-travel journey where they meet historical figures in humorous situations.

Bedtime Invention Story: Create a story about a young inventor who comes up with hilarious and impractical contraptions.

Bedtime Giggle Story: Incorporate funny sound effects, silly voices, and tickle breaks throughout the story. Remember, the key is to have fun and let your imagination run wild.

These funny bedtime storytelling techniques can make the bedtime routine an enjoyable and memorable experience for both kids and parents.

The Hilarious Grandparent Handbook

Here's a list of classic children's books with a humorous twist for reading aloud:

"Where the Wild Things Are" by Maurice Sendak - Read it with silly monster voices and exaggerated roars.

"The Cat in the Hat" by Dr. Seuss - Embrace the charming chaos with enthusiasm.

"Winnie the Pooh" by A.A. Milne - Add comical voices for each character, especially Tigger and Eeyore.

"Alice's Adventures in Wonderland" by Lewis Carroll - Emphasize the whimsical absurdity of Wonderland.

"Matilda" by Roald Dahl - Capture the humor in Matilda's clever antics and Miss Trunchbull's over-the-top villainy.

"Charlie and the Chocolate Factory" by Roald Dahl - Bring out the eccentricities of Willy Wonka and the Golden Ticket winners.

"James and the Giant Peach" by Roald Dahl - Convey the quirky personalities of the insect characters.

"The BFG" by Roald Dahl - Give the Big Friendly Giant a fun, distinct voice and play with the quirky Giant-speak.

"The Stinky Cheese Man and Other Fairly Stupid Tales" by Jon Scieszka and Lane Smith - A collection of hilarious fractured fairy tales.

"The True Story of the Three Little Pigs" by Jon Scieszka and Lane Smith - Offer a different perspective on the classic story.

The Hilarious Grandparent Handbook

"Cloudy with a Chance of Meatballs" by Judi Barrett - Add humor by describing the outlandish food weather.

"If You Give a Mouse a Cookie" by Laura Numeroff - Highlight the absurd chain of events when the mouse gets a cookie.

"Don't Let the Pigeon Drive the Bus!" by Mo Willems - Make the pigeon's pleas and tantrums entertaining. "The Paper Bag Princess" by Robert Munsch - Embrace the spunky humor as the princess outwits a dragon.

"Goodnight Moon" by Margaret Wise Brown - Create a silly bedtime ritual with humorous goodnight wishes.

"Green Eggs and Ham" by Dr. Seuss - Emphasize the stubbornness of the character who won't try the green eggs and ham.

"The Day the Crayons Quit" by Drew Daywalt - Use different voices for each crayon's complaint letters.

"Llama Llama Red Pajama" by Anna Dewdney - Make Llama's bedtime drama amusing and relatable.

"Diary of a Wimpy Kid" by Jeff Kinney - Read aloud Greg Heffley's hilarious and relatable diary entries.

Reading these classic children's books with a humorous twist can make storytime even more enjoyable for kids and adults alike. Let your imagination run wild and have fun bringing these tales to life with laughter and funny voices!

The Hilarious Grandparent Handbook

Chapter 7: Grandparent Adventures

Create unforgettable memories with your grandkids by going on hilarious adventures together.

Whether it's a trip to the local zoo or a daring escapade in your own backyard, we've got you covered with adventure ideas that'll have everyone in stitches.

The Hilarious Grandparent Handbook

Nature Scavenger Hunt: Create a list of items in nature, like a pinecone, a ladybug, or a feather, who can find them first.

Leaf Pile Olympics: Rake up a big pile of leaves competitions like who can jump the farthest or do the funniest somersault into the pile.

Rock Painting: Collect some smooth rocks and paint funny faces or designs on them, then hide them in the garden for a rock hunt.

Bubble Bonanza: Bring out a bubble wand and have a contest to see who can blow the biggest or wackiest bubble.

Bug Safari: Explore the backyard with a magnifying glass and see who can find the most interesting bugs.

Picnic with a Twist: Have a picnic but pack some surprising and silly foods like gummy worms, cotton candy, or cheeseburgers.

Nature Art: Collect leaves, sticks, and flowers to create funny and imaginative nature art.

Water Balloon Fights: On a hot day, engage in a water balloon battle with your grandkids.

Birdwatching: Set up a bird feeder and watch the birds together. Try to identify different species and make up funny names for them.

The Hilarious Grandparent Handbook

Cloud Shapes: Lie on a blanket and look up at the clouds, making up funny stories about the shapes you see. Make a

Mini Obstacle Course: Create a small obstacle course with items from around the yard and see who can complete it the fastest.

Gardening with a Twist: Plant funny-shaped vegetables or fruits like square watermelons or heart-shaped carrots.

Nature Puppets: Use sticks, leaves, and other natural materials to create puppets and put on a funny puppet show.

Geocaching: Go on a treasure hunt by geocaching in a nearby park or nature reserve. It's like a real-life treasure hunt using GPS coordinates.

Sidewalk Chalk Art: Draw funny and colorful pictures on the driveway or sidewalk.

Tin Can Telephone: Make a tin can telephone and have a giggle-filled conversation with your grandkids from different ends of the yard.

Camping in the Backyard: Set up a tent and camp out in the backyard, telling funny stories and stargazing.

Funny Costume Parade: Have a costume parade where everyone dresses up in the silliest costumes they can find.

The Hilarious Grandparent Handbook

Outdoor Movie Night: Project a funny movie on a screen outdoors and enjoy popcorn and snacks under the stars.

Bike or Scooter Race: Organize a race around the block or down a local trail and award funny prizes for different categories.

Remember, the most important thing is to have fun and create lasting memories together.

These outdoor adventures will not only bring laughter but also strengthen the bond between grandparents and their grandkids.

The Hilarious Grandparent Handbook

Chapter 8: The Grandparent Dance-Off

Break out the moves and challenge your grandkids to a dance-off.

We'll help you pick the perfect dance anthem and teach you some classic and contemporary moves to ensure you don't lose the title of "Coolest Grandparent" any time soon.

The Hilarious Grandparent Handbook

"The Hip Swivel": Stand with your feet shoulder-width apart and gently swivel your hips from side to side. Imagine you're stirring a giant pot of soup with your hips. Add a big smile for extra flair!

"The Shuffle and Shake": Take small steps to the side and shuffle your feet while shaking your arms like you're trying to shake off water. This move is both fun and a good workout!

"The Knee-Knocking Boogie": Lift one knee at a time and knock them together in time with the music. It's like a silly twist on traditional knee lifts.

"The Invisible Hula Hoop": Pretend you're hula hooping, but without an actual hoop. Circle your hips as if you're keeping an invisible hula hoop in motion. You can even challenge your dance partner to join in on the imaginary fun!

"The Flap and Clap": Stand with your feet apart and flap your arms like a bird trying to take off, then follow it with some enthusiastic clapping. This combo is sure to bring laughter to the dance floor.

"The Robot Granny/Grandpa": Dance with stiff, robotic movements, and then suddenly transition to fluid, funky moves. It's a playful nod to the classic robot dance but with your own unique twist.

The Hilarious Grandparent Handbook

"The Speedy Gonzales": Take small, fast steps in place while waving your arms like you're trying to catch a runaway mouse. This one's all about quick, comical footwork. "The

Disco Dentures": Pretend to take out imaginary dentures and wave them in the air while you keep grooving. It's a humorous take on the classic disco moves.

"The Gardening Groove": Pretend you're planting seeds while dancing. Reach down, pick up imaginary seeds, plant them, and then water your dance floor garden with some funky watering can moves.

"The Rocking Rocker": Sit in a chair, pretend you're rocking in a rocking chair, and sway your upper body back and forth. This is perfect for those moments when you want to take a seated dance break. Remember, the key is to have fun and let loose on the dance floor.

These dance moves are all about embracing your inner child and enjoying the moment. So, put on some music, invite your grandkids to join, and dance like nobody's watching!

The Hilarious Grandparent Handbook

Chapter 9: When All Else Fails – The Grandparent Handbook for Sanity

Let's face it, being a grandparent can be exhausting. In this chapter, we'll offer some tips and tricks for maintaining your sanity when the grandkids are running wild.

Sometimes you just need a little humor and a lot of patience.

The Hilarious Grandparent Handbook

Invest in Noise-Canceling Earmuffs:

For those times when their laughter turns into a cacophony of chaos. Embrace "Grandma's Time-Out Corner":

Designate a comfy chair as your sanctuary. When things get wild, retreat there and pretend you're on a tropical vacation.

Hire a Kid Whisperer: Have a friend who's exceptionally good with children on speed dial. They can come over for reinforcements when things get extra crazy.

Stock Up on Chocolate and Coffee: These are your secret sanity saviors. Sneak chocolate bites and caffeine shots when they're not looking.

Join Their Games: Show them that you can be wild too! Dress up in a ridiculous costume and join their imaginary adventures.

Master the Art of "Grandpa Jokes": Dole out dad jokes liberally. Kids will be too busy groaning to cause trouble.

Learn the "Naptime Jedi Mind Trick": Convince them that taking a nap is a superpower, and they'll gladly take a snooze break.

The Hilarious Grandparent Handbook

Create a "No Grown-Ups Allowed" Club:

Pretend you're not allowed in their secret clubhouse. Watch them try to keep you out. DIY Confetti Cannon: Keep one handy for special occasions (like successfully surviving a wild grandkid day).

Install a "Kid-Friendly" Speed Bump: A strategically placed laundry basket can slow down their rampaging horde. Declare "Grandma Dance Party" Hours:

Put on your dancing shoes and challenge them to dance-offs. Tired kids are well- behaved kids! Adopt a Grandparent Pet Rock: Whenever you need a breather, confide in your pet rock. It's an excellent listener.

Create the "Clean-Up Race": Tell them the fastest cleanup crew wins a prize (and make the prize a high-five or an extra cookie).

Host "Guess the Mystery Smell" Challenges: Blindfold them and have them guess what's cooking in the kitchen. The winner gets a kitchen tour.

Implement the "Grandkids Dictate Dinner" Night: Let them design the menu. Mac and cheese with a side of ice cream, anyone?

Designate a "Grandkid Referee Shirt": Wear it proudly, and whenever chaos erupts, blow a whistle and make a ruling.

The Hilarious Grandparent Handbook

Play Hide and Seek with the TV Remote:

Hours of entertainment watching them hunt for the remote (make sure you remember where you hid it).

Fake Grandma's Rules Book: Pretend you have an ancient book of rules, and "consult" it for answers to their questions.

Invent Silly Superhero Names: Give them superhero identities and let them create wild superhero stories. The "Grandparent Double Agent" Trick: Secretly side with one grandkid against the others and watch the hilarity unfold.

 Remember, humor can be a great tool for surviving the chaos of grandkids running wild. Laughter is the best medicine, and it can help maintain your sanity while making wonderful memories with your grandkids.

The Hilarious Grandparent Handbook

Chapter 10: The Grand Finale – Leaving a Legacy of Laughter

Discover how to leave a lasting legacy of love, laughter, and wisdom for your grandkids.

We'll share ideas for creating a "Grandparent Time Capsule" and other sentimental gifts that will be cherished for generations to come.

The Hilarious Grandparent Handbook

Personal Stories and Memories: Share stories from your life and family history.

Create a written or recorded memoir, so your grandchildren can learn about their roots and the experiences that shaped your family.

Family Recipe Book: Compile a cookbook with family recipes that have been passed down through generations. Include personal notes and anecdotes about the recipes and their significance.

Handwritten Letters: Write heartfelt letters to your grandchildren, expressing your love, wisdom, and hopes for their future. These letters can be kept as treasured mementos.

Photo Albums and Videos: Create photo albums or video recordings documenting family gatherings, special occasions, and everyday life. Include captions or voiceovers to explain the context and stories behind the images.

Personalized Gifts: Consider giving your grandchildren personalized items like handcrafted quilts, blankets, or other handmade crafts that have sentimental value.

The Hilarious Grandparent Handbook

Savings or Investments: Start a savings account or investment fund for your grandchildren's education or future needs. This can be a financial legacy to support their goals.

Educational Support:
Offer to pay for your grandchildren's education or set up a college fund to help them pursue their academic aspirations.

Heirlooms and Treasures:
Pass down family heirlooms, such as jewelry, furniture, or other cherished possessions, along with the stories and history behind these items.

Philanthropy and Charitable Giving:
Encourage a sense of social responsibility by making a donation to a charity or establishing a family foundation in your name, or jointly with your grandchildren.

Teach Life Skills:
Spend time teaching your grandchildren valuable life skills, such as gardening, cooking, or woodworking. Pass on your knowledge and experience to help them become self-sufficient.

Family Traditions:
Share and establish family traditions that can be carried on

for generations. Whether it's a special holiday ritual, a family reunion, or a shared hobby, these traditions create a strong bond.

The Hilarious Grandparent Handbook

Educational and Inspirational Books: Gift books that have had a significant impact on your life or that you believe offer valuable lessons and insights for your grandchildren.

Personalized Advice:

Write a letter or create a video offering advice and guidance on important life topics, such as relationships, career, and personal development.

Record Your Family Tree:

Create a detailed family tree or genealogy chart that traces your family's lineage back several generations, including information about your ancestors.

Encourage Hobbies and Passions:

Support your grandchildren's interests and hobbies by providing resources, lessons, or equipment related to their passions.

Time and Attention:

Spend quality time with your grandchildren, sharing your experiences, values, and life lessons. Your presence and guidance can be a priceless legacy.

Document Life Lessons:

Record your life lessons, values, and principles in a personal journal or a video series that can be passed down to your grandchildren.

The Hilarious Grandparent Handbook

College or Career Mentoring: Offer guidance and mentorship to help your grandchildren make informed decisions about their education and career paths.

Preserve Cultural Heritage: Pass down cultural traditions, languages, and customs that are important to your family's heritage.

Encourage a Love for Nature: Share your appreciation for the natural world by taking your grandchildren on outdoor adventures, teaching them about the environment, and instilling a love for nature.

Leaving a legacy is about creating lasting memories, imparting knowledge, and building a strong emotional connection with your grandchildren.

These gifts of legacy can help ensure that your influence and love continue to shape their lives for years to come.

The Hilarious Grandparent Handbook

Grandparent Time Capsule

Letters and Notes: Handwritten letters from the grandparents to their grandchildren, sharing life advice, personal anecdotes, and well wishes.
Letters or cards written by the grandchildren to their grandparents.

Family Photos: A selection of family photos, including pictures of the
grandparents when they were young, wedding photos, family gatherings, and photos of the grandchildren.

A family tree or genealogy chart.
Personal Memorabilia:

Treasured heirlooms such as jewelry, watches, or other items with sentimental value.

Grandparents' favorite books, recipes, or music albums.
A piece of clothing or accessory that represents the grandparents' style.

Keepsakes:
Grandchildren's artwork, crafts, or school projects.
Special items or mementos from the grandchildren, like a lock of hair, baby clothes, or their favorite toys.

The Hilarious Grandparent Handbook

Technology and Media: A flash drive or digital storage device with video messages, voice recordings, or digital diaries from the grandparents.

A video recording of the grandparents sharing their life stories, experiences, and family history.

Newspapers and Magazines: Current newspapers or magazines from the year of the time capsule's creation to show historical context.

Written Memories: Journals or diaries kept by the grandparents, detailing their daily lives, experiences, and thoughts.

Family Recipes: Handwritten or printed family recipes, along with a sample of a favorite dish or treat.

Milestones and Achievements: Certificates, awards, or recognition received by the grandparents or the grandchildren.

The Hilarious Grandparent Handbook

News and World Events: A summary of significant world events, local news, or personal reflections on the year when the time capsule is sealed.

Technology and Trends: Include items like old cell phones, tablets, or gadgets that were popular during the grandparents' time to show technological changes.

Family Traditions and Stories: Descriptions of family traditions, customs, and memorable stories that have been passed down through generations.

A Letter to the Future: A heartfelt letter from the grandparents addressed to their future generations, offering wisdom, love, and hopes for the family's future.

Sealing Ceremony: A video or photographs of the grandparents and grandchildren sealing the time capsule.

A Will or Legal Documents: If desired, include copies of important legal documents, wills, or estate plans for reference. Location Information:

A map or description of the location where the time capsule is buried or stored, along with instructions for when it should be opened.

Remember to use a sturdy and airtight container for the time capsule to protect its contents from the elements. Ensure that it's stored in a safe and memorable location, and consider setting a specific date or occasion for its opening, such as a milestone birthday or a family reunion, to pass on the legacy and love of the grandparents to future generations.

The Hilarious Grandparent Handbook

Steve Lewis

Dear Reader, Thank you for picking up a copy of "The Hilarious Grandparent Handbook." We hope you've enjoyed this delightful and heartwarming journey into the world of grandparenthood.

Whether you're a grandparent yourself, about to become one, or simply curious about the joys and quirks of this unique role, we appreciate your time and interest in our book.

Writing "The Hilarious Grandparent Handbook" has been a labor of love, and our goal was to capture the essence of what it means to be a grandparent in a way that celebrates the laughter, wisdom, and pure joy that comes with the territory.

We wanted to provide a light-hearted and humorous guide to help you navigate the often unpredictable, yet incredibly rewarding, world of grandparenting. We would like to extend our gratitude to the many grandparents, parents, and children who shared their stories, wisdom, and anecdotes with us.

Your personal experiences and insights have enriched the pages of this book and made it more authentic and relatable to readers of all backgrounds.

The Hilarious Grandparent Handbook

Steve Lewis

We hope that you've found "The Hilarious Grandparent Handbook" to be a source of laughter, inspiration, and perhaps a few "Aha!" moments.

Grandparenting is a unique adventure, and we encourage you to embrace it with open arms and a hearty sense of humor.

If you've enjoyed your reading journey with us, please consider sharing your thoughts in a review or recommending this book to friends and family. Your support means the world to us, and it helps other readers discover the joys of grandparenthood through the pages of this handbook.

Once again, thank you for choosing "The Hilarious Grandparent Handbook" as your reading companion. We wish you countless joyful moments with your grandkids and an abundance of laughter in your grandparenting adventures. With warm regards and heartfelt thanks, Steve Lewis

Notes

Notes

Printed in Great Britain
by Amazon